A Strange Place to Sing

written by
TERRY WHALIN

illustrated by **ANDY STILES**

STANDARD
PUBLISHING
Cincinnati, Ohio

"My heart leaps for joy
and I will give thanks
to him in song."
Psalm 28:7

The Standard Publishing Company, Cincinnati, Ohio
A division of Standex International Corporation
© 1994 by The Standard Publishing Company
All rights reserved.
Printed in the United States of America
01 00 99 98 97 96 95 94   5 4 3 2 1
Library of Congress Catalog Number 94-7171
Cataloging-in-Publication data available
ISBN 0-7847-0273-X

Designed by Coleen Davis

Paul and Silas were in big-time trouble . . .

The problem began when Paul and Silas
came to the town of Philippi.
They were telling people about Jesus, God's Son.

But some people didn't like Paul and Silas. These men said Paul and Silas were doing bad things — even though they weren't.

The men hauled Paul and Silas before the judges of the town.

"These two should be in jail," the men said. "We don't like what they are doing."

The crowd shouted, "Yeah. Toss them into jail!"

"We agree," said the judges. "Take them away and lock them up!"

The soldiers beat Paul and Silas
and dragged them off to prison.

"Guard these men carefully," they told the jailer.
"If they escape, it will be your fault."

The jailer took Paul and Silas deep into the prison.

Paul and Silas were alone.
It was too dark to see anything.
Their bodies hurt,
and they couldn't move.

They could have been very sad and even angry — but they weren't.

What a strange place
to sing!
People in prison
usually cried
and moaned.

The other prisoners were surprised.
They listened to every word.
Even in the middle of the night,
Paul and Silas were still praying and singing,
praising God.

The prisoners' chains rattled and fell off, and all the doors popped open.

When the shaking stopped,
the jailer ran in and saw all the open doors.
My prisoners have escaped! he thought.
I am in terrible trouble now.
The jailer pulled out his sword.

The jailer couldn't believe it.
He called for a light.
Then he dropped on his knees
in front of Paul and Silas.
"I heard you singing," he said.
"How can I be saved?"

"Believe on the Lord Jesus," said Paul and Silas.
"Then you will be saved, and your whole family."

The jailer did believe in Jesus.
His family did too.
Paul and Silas baptized them all.

Then, with great joy,
everyone ate a meal together.

In the morning, the judges let Paul and Silas go.

"But you must leave our town," the judges said.

Paul and Silas said good-bye to the jailer and his family.

Then they left, happy that God had used their singing — even in a very strange place!